7-year-muse

JM Marasigan

Presentation by *BookLeaf Publishing*

Web: www.bookleafpub.com

E-mail: info@bookleafpub.com

ISBN : 9789357699402

First edition 2022

DEDICATION

For Mom and Casey.

2:31 pm

nothing but thoughts and the endless cold,
to keep me company.
got a pen and a paper,
hoping writing to you would rescue me,
from the loneliness I feel,
holding on to your lingering memories.
I feel so homeless, helpless.
I know you're not my home and you won't save me.
I guess there's magic cause having you in my thoughts
somehow calms me,
soothes me,
and comforts me.
we barely talk and you don't know who I am.
I'm in love with you, it's funny to think, I really am.
I can't wait for the day till I see you again,
for now, I'm thankful for what we have,
happy to be your friend.

Coffee.

somehow, I wish you knew this side of me,
that I wasn't just someone you see,
and things that you heard or know about me.
I wasn't as mediocre or shallow,
I'm not who you think I am but to reveal myself
would ruin me,
for what you thought was nothing close to "I".
so, for once, please just take some time to really
figure me out.
know me like it's the first time we've met,
ask me what my passions are and what I do best,
make me feel I'm worthy of your time.
for once, please just be someone who'd show
interest
and really mean it,
I know I'm not much but maybe,
if you take much effort and time.
then maybe you'd see things in my perspective,
maybe you'd want to know more and see more
with me.
to cut this short, please just have coffee with me.

SIX

6 months and forever ago,
you walked right at my door,
managed to break all the walls,
I've built down the hall.
You spoke a language,
only you and I understood.
I knew how it would end
but I wanted to somehow pretend.
Late night drives, sneaking in
and sneaking out again.
Love is such a cruel thing,
I hear our clock ticking
Again, and again.
One of the most painful things,
is to either hold on or let go
of a love that's doomed
from the beginning.

Photographs

As I scroll through my gallery,
I saw an old photograph of you and me,
Smiling awkwardly with you sitting next to me.
Remembering that moment so vividly.
Wishing we could go back to that exact memory.
When life was simple, not much to worry.
I'd give everything to see you again,
To capture that moment where it all began.
Travel back in time,
Whispering "God, I wish you were mine."

C

I met you once at a coffee shop 7 years ago, to be
exact.
ever since I fell for you, I haven't stopped.
To say you're beautiful is an understatement.
You are so much more than that.
Your burning passion in what you do,
that sparkle in your eyes,
talking about the things that you love.
I tried to know you more...
For you, I tried to be enough,
But the timing was never right,
a chance for us was never in sight.
I stopped trying but I never gave up,
I knew one day I had to push my luck.
Praying someday you might come back.
We'll both be at the same place at the same time.
Uncertain, endlessly hoping that would be
enough.

I'm sorry.

do you know how hard I try for "us" to happen?
for the possibility of us being together,
it's hard to keep trying if every day,
you make me feel like I'm never going to be a
part
of your plan.
to your long list of priorities, I'll never be one.
I never even had the chance,
you never gave me one.
I guess all I wanted to tell you was,
there was once a time when
I tried my hardest to keep you around,
but it wasn't enough,
I wasn't enough.
I'm sorry if you can't give me a chance.
I'm sorry I needed you, but you didn't need me
back.
I'm sorry I wanted you to want me like I want
you.
I'm sorry I couldn't stick around much longer,
I'll forever think of you and the chance we never
had.

MOON

you told me you've been craving for someone's
touch,
that very look and feel of having someone to
love,
yet you flinch every time someone gets close
enough,
that thought of committing your soul to another,
for you, is a trap
danger, you say,
you push them away,
before you get too attached,
inviting their souls just to sell it away,
making a heart swoon just to leave it today,
you act so innocent and brave,
yet you break hearts just by hiding yours away.
stop this wolf from crying,
let it touch your love worth waiting,
let me show you a risk worth taking,
give a chance, you won't regret.
a story of love, you won't for a second, forget.

SIGNS

I don't know what happened,
how it started,
how it ended,
how you reappeared,
and disappeared once again.
in retrospect, I know I should've done better.
I should've said the right words when it
mattered.
I should've asked how you were doing
instead of where we're going.
I should've paid more attention
rather than proving my intentions
I guess I should've focused on the obvious signs
rather than lying to myself,
trying to make you mine,
I just hope you're fine,
please know that even if we don't talk,
you have never left my mind.

CROSS PATHS

9

the truth is I know it was never meant to be
you were never meant for me,
i have blinded myself with hope,
now I don't know how to cope,
all I have are fading memories,
along with this unending misery,
forgive me for asking more than you can give,
for wishing I could take more than I can receive,
today I accept that we cross paths for a reason,
it was a long journey, thank you for being there
for
a season.

That time at the lake

i wanted to write about this day,
i felt like you were there,
although you were 7,000 miles away.
i promised myself i'd bring you there one day.
i wish it would be easier to ask you to run away,
if I can make you smile,
would that make it worth your while?
if I didn't ruin that night,
would I have done alright?
if you were with me at the lake,
would I be able to make up for my mistake?
i know you won't remember,
it happened last December.
that was my first lie,
it was around July.
i know this is late,
i do apologize,
for making you wait.

With you,
I feel a feeling I've never felt.
With you,
I can't see a future with anyone else.
With you,
I feel something different,
something that might never end.
Will you and I ever make sense?
Wishing someday I would be worthy,
I'll wait till we're 30.
When you're not too busy,
please come and see me.
If fates allow, I'd be so happy.
I will love you till over 60.

Mom

I know I don't say these words enough,
I owe you everything,
Who I am today,
I miss you; I love you and I wish I could see
you.
You are the reason I am here,
I'm forever grateful for you,
You are the light that guides me in the dark,
You are all the reasons
That's keeping me alive.
I owe you a lifetime of apology
For being the cause of your pain and misery.
Once I come home, I promise to make it up.
For now, please know you are the best mother
anyone could ever have.
I'll always regret not giving you that last hug
when
you asked,
As I close my eyes,
I see that actual flashback.
Till then, thank you for always having my back.

Feel better.

I am writing to you again,
since we don't speak.
I've been meaning to ask how you're doing
since last week.
heard you have it rough these days…
stay tough, dark times fade away…
still one of the strongest people I know,
one of the many reasons I adore.
we all have those days when we feel like the
worse.
you know too well it would pass,
those too aren't built to last.
i'm here if you need a friend.
someone who will listen,
someone who will understand.
these are all I could offer,
still wishing I was closer,
when these things happen,
I wish I could hold her,
for just a moment,
maybe I can help her feel better.

Life in backwards

14

Lately I found myself looking back,
Instead of moving forward,
I keep stepping back,
I'm walking behind the tracks,
Following the wrong path.
Left thinking about the past,
I don't know how to make things last.
They always say, "This too shall pass."
I know it's not the way to live,
Is it my fault, people always leave?

07.05.21

I closed my eyes,
I'm back in Cali,
over a thousand miles away,
Did you miss me?
I remember that smile,
I'd kill for another time,
to talk for hours,
that night was ours.
to hear your voice,
above my heartbeat noise.
You won't remember,
and I never forget,
that July laughter,
moments, I will never regret.

Sometimes.

sometimes it's easier to fantasize
over things,
over you,
over us.
sometimes i just look at my phone,
seeing messages from you that I never reCeived.
sAying how much I mean to you
and how the little thingS I do lights up your
facE.
i sometimes see You beside Me in the morning,
sleeping quietlY, calm, dReaming like a child.
dreaming like me, together we'd cuddle
and soon we'd wake and face the day,
neVer forgetting about havIng breakfast together.
driNking coffee And that's how we start our
day...
with a coffee date.
i'Ll drop you off to work and say "hi." to some
of
your students,
you'll kiss me goodbye,
you won't say goodbye,
you know it's always going to be "See you
later!"
these are just dreams,
imaginations, and illusions.

lord knows how I wanted everything to be real,
for an "us" to be real,
for a ChANce to make iT reAl.
one day,
we will meet again,
Right time,
right plAce...
right, love?

The end

let's start at the end...
you don't have to do anything,
you don't have to say something,
we both know since the beginning...
I'm more to losing than winning.
so, let's start at the end,
help this broken heart mend.
you disappeared once again,
will you ever come back?
please, lie and pretend.

Our universe

Say the words I long to hear,
please whisper in my ear,
I'm glad to have you here,
forever wishing you were near.
A two-letter word
will haunt you when it's told.
"No." she said as she leaves me in the cold.
Shivers quietly, broken dreams of growing old
together.
I plead politely "Don't go!"
Don't leave me hanging out in the woods,
Left with "could've been"
"might've been"
Hoping she would
change her mind,
One day she will find
"Us."
somewhere,
in our own universe.
Humming to the melody,
while I sing our last verse.

Muse

/myooz/

A person or personified force who is the source
of inspiration for a creative artist.

I can't thank you enough.
You're the only comfort
when times get tough.
Your thoughts echo in my head,
helps me get out of bed.
You keep me sane,
in a place that has gone insane.
You make me look forward to the future,
that remains unsure.
You are the best reminder,
that life could be better.
The world deserves more "yous."
No matter what happens,
It's been an absolute pleasure
having you as my muse.

Untitled

Please don't run.
In another life,
Hold my hand
One day
You
Will
Get a chance,
If I ever,
Give up
Will you
Be there
If I can't
Be enough
Would I
Matter less
You will never
See,
You
Like
I do.